# Intern Insider

Internships have all but become a requirement when starting out in the fields of entertainment and broadcasting. Students need these internships not only to get their foot in the door, but to gain valuable experience that gives them an advantage when going for that first job in the industry. *Intern Insider* helps students navigate the often daunting task of finding an internship, and equips readers to use the experience learned to begin a strong career in the entertainment world.

As both a professional broadcaster and college professor, author Tammy Trujillo approaches the topic of internships from both sides: what the student and intern site hope to gain. She provides various valuable perspectives throughout the book, including student assessments on their internship experiences, case studies of those who have turned their internships into careers, and interviews with internship site coordinators. Her breadth of knowledge and experience make for a ground-level book both informative and useful.

In the competitive landscape of today's entertainment and broadcasting worlds, *Intern Insider* provides students with all the tools they need to make the most of their internships and jumpstart their careers!

**Tammy Trujillo** is both an entertainer and an educator. She began in the entertainment field as a child and since graduating from Cal State Fullerton, has continuously worked in the Los Angeles market as a News Anchor, Reporter, Sportscaster and Commercial Voiceover Artist. Combining her real-world experience with a hands-on approach to learning, Tammy has also taught broadcasting for the past 25 years at many of Southern California's most prestigious private schools and colleges. She is currently the lead Professor of Broadcasting at Mt. San Antonio College, as well as Director of its two award-winning campus radio stations. Throughout her career, she has received numerous honors for her work both on the air and behind-the-scenes, including several Golden Mike Awards from the Radio Television News Association. Tammy is a member of SAG-AFTRA, in the Long Beach City Hall of Fame, a member of Pacific Pioneer Broadcasters and a former Board member of the Associated Press Television Radio Assocation.

# Intern Insider

## Getting the Most Out of Your Internship in the Entertainment Field

Tammy Trujillo

Routledge
Taylor & Francis Group

NEW YORK AND LONDON

First published 2016
by Routledge
711 Third Avenue, New York, NY 10017

and by Routledge
2 Park Square, Milton Park, Abingdon, Oxon, OX14 4RN

*Routledge is an imprint of the Taylor & Francis Group, an informa business*

© 2016 Taylor & Francis

*Library of Congress Cataloging in Publication Data*
Names: Trujillo, Tammy, author.
Title: Intern insider : getting the most out of your internship in the
entertainment field / Tammy Trujillo.
Description: New York, NY ; Abingdon, Oxon : Routledge, 2016.
Identifiers: LCCN 2015046224 (print) | LCCN 2016000529 (ebook) |
ISBN 9781138659384 (hardback) | ISBN 9781138925472 (pbk.) |
ISBN 9781315620251 (ebook)
Subjects: LCSH: Mass media—Study and teaching (Internship)—
United States. | Performing arts—Study and teaching (Internship)—
United States.
Classification: LCC n-us— (print) | LCC P91.5.U5 (ebook) |
DDC 791.07155—dc23
LC record available at http://lccn.loc.gov/2015046224

ISBN: 978-1-138-65938-4 (hbk)
ISBN: 978-1-138-92547-2 (pbk)
ISBN: 978-1-315-62025-1 (ebk)

Typeset in Bembo
by Florence Production Ltd, Stoodleigh, Devon, UK

# Contents

**PART 3**

**During the Internship**      **65**

**PART 4**

**After the Internship**      **93**

# Introduction

Congratulations! You are about to embark on one of the most exciting adventures in your quest to work in the entertainment field.

Many jobs are now requiring students to have done at least one and sometimes two internships before entering the workforce. Employers see internships as a way of weeding out people who aren't really serious about the industry. They're also a way of "seasoning" people who will go on to apply and hopefully get entry-level positions.

An internship is really like being handed the keys to the kingdom. It's your chance to go where most people only dream about. You'll actually be going inside a radio station, on the set of a TV show or movie, inside a recording studio or production house.

This book is designed to take you from finding an internship and preparing for an interview to landing the gig and making the most of the experience.

So get ready to make a lasting impression and get started on your career!

# Part I

# Before the Internship

# Chapter 1

# Become an Intern!
# The Value of Real-World
# Experience!

- Understanding the Purpose of the Internship
- What is an Internship?
- Putting What You Learned in the Classroom Into Practice

What exactly is an internship? That is something that is currently under review by our legal system. The question is: when does work being done stop being an internship and become an actual job, which under Federal Labor Law has to result in the person being paid at least the minimum wage and overtime compensation for any hours over 40 worked within a workweek.

There are certain circumstances where people can work at "for-profit" companies without being paid. This applies to interns who receive training for their own education benefit, if the training meets a set of six criteria developed by the United States Department of Labor, Wage and Hour Division:

- The internship, even though it includes actual operation of the facilities of the employer, is similar to training, which would be given in an educational environment;
- The internship experience is for the benefit of the intern;
- The intern does not displace regular employees, but works under close supervision of the existing staff;

- The employer that provides the training derives no immediate advantage from the activities of the intern; and on occasion its operations may actually be impeded;
- The intern is not necessarily entitled to a job at the conclusion of the internship; and
- The employer and the intern understand that the intern is not entitled to wages for the time spent in the internship.

If all six of these criteria are met, it means that under The Fair Labor Standards Act, an employment relationship does not exist and the Act's rules on minimum wage and overtime do not apply.

Boiled down, it means that as an intern:

- You have more to learn before you are ready for a job and the training you will get at your internship is similar to what you would get in a classroom setting;
- You are benefiting from doing the internship, not the company. While you may contribute to the company by what you do at your internship, you doing it or being there is not vital to the company;
- No one was fired or moved to make room for you at the company and you are working under close supervision of people already employed by the company;
- The company is not getting a benefit from the work that you do and in some cases having to take time out to work with you actually slows down the overall progress of the company;
- There is no guarantee the company will hire you at the end of your internship. It doesn't mean the company can't hire you, there is just no promise of them doing so; and
- That both you and the company understand that you are not getting paid for the time you spend at the company.

Part of the problems that have surfaced recently involving interns is that some companies were having their interns do work that really should have been done by a paid employee, and if there was too much work for the actual employees to do, then another person should have been hired to take up the slack. This concept is called "supplanting", meaning the act of using an intern to take the place of a paid employee. This clearly violates the Fair Labor Standards Act.

Working your way through the requirements for a college degree or certificate is similar to putting a jigsaw puzzle together. How some of the pieces fit together is pretty obvious; others look more like they belong to something else. In some cases, you really don't know what the final picture will be until the last pieces fall into place.

An internship is where it all starts to come together. It's the link between a classroom setting and the real world. An internship is your first chance to see how the classes that may have seemed unrelated actually make sense in a real world workplace. You finally get to walk through the door of an actual studio, station or set and see how the professionals do the jobs that you have been so anxious to do.

An internship is an opportunity to test what you have learned in the classroom and take your education to a new and crucial level. It's a way to measure how ready you are to enter the workforce and to determine what skills you still need to develop and which ones just need a little polishing. And, you'll get your first taste or what it's like to work in the entertainment industry on a daily basis as you discover what actually goes on behind-the-scenes.

That's a very important reason many entry-level employers want you to have done at least one internship. As a consumer of the entertainment field up until this point in your life, you've probably only seen the final product. That's all we're supposed to see in that capacity. After all, you wouldn't want to go to a play and have the actors come out before it begins and tell you how many long, hard days they put into rehearsals. You just want to see and enjoy the final product. But if you are going to work in the industry, you need to know what the job fully entails.

Your internship is a kind of an "introduction" to the business . . . an opportunity to get over the perceived glitz and glam of the industry so that when you get your first paid job, you understand what is going on, and are ready to handle it.

But there is a big difference between an internship and that first job. While you will have to beat out a great many other people to get the position, and you need to treat it with the same commitment that you would an actual job, an internship comes without one major component . . . a paycheck. There are very few internships that pay a salary but most do require that you are enrolled in a college program where you will be getting credit for the work you do. While the credit is nice, the real-world, hands-on experience that you will be getting is your real pay.

You will also have the semester to show everyone at your internship site just what you do have to offer. Think of it as a semester-long audition. While a relatively small percentage of internships result in a job offer at their conclusion—the national average is about 37 percent—they can result in a recommendation, and as a future connection for a job down the line.

Not all colleges offer internship programs. And in the case of many that do, the per-credit fee can be rather high. A good idea is to check with your local community or two-year colleges to see if they have a program and if you can get in it. The cost is certainly going to be lower.

You may find though that some professors are reluctant to allow you in since you didn't study at that college and they don't know you, your abilities, or your work ethic. When you apply as an intern, you're representing the college program that will be giving you credit for your internship and no one wants to burn any bridges in the industry. In a way, the college is putting its stamp of approval on you saying that you are ready to be involved in a professional setting. If this is the case, explain your situation and offer to show some of your work to the person in charge of the program. You may be able to overcome that objection and get into the class.

While it might be tempting to work at an internship, even if you have not found a way to get college credit for doing so, as a way of "getting your foot in the door", you should not do it. The bottom line is that it is illegal.

If you are lucky enough to find a paid internship, you must be paid at least minimum wage and taxes will be taken out of your check, just like they would be at any other job. The company cannot pay you less than the minimum wage under the guise that you are "just" an intern and are essentially engaged in on-the-job training.

The company can reimburse you for certain expenses. You don't need to pay for things out of your pocket as a way of showing what a good team player you are. If you are asked to get coffee, then you should be given the money up front to buy it. If you are sent on a company-related errand and have to pay to park in a lot, then get the receipt and bring it back for reimbursement. If you use your own car to do a task for the company, then you should be compensated for the gas you used in doing so. Make a note of your miles from the station and back again. There is a standard mileage fee that the company should use to determine how much money is owed you.

## POINTS TO REMEMBER

- You are not working for free, you are being paid in real-world experience.
- Even though you are not being paid in cash, you need to treat your internship like you would any other job.
- You will likely need to be enrolled in a college program that will give you credit for your internship.
- Be realistic about your skill level going into the internship and what you need to learn or perfect.

# Chapter 2

# Who Would Want to Hire Me? There's Nothing Interesting on my Resumé!

- How to Assess Your Skills and Abilities
- How to Prepare Your Introduction Material
- Get Your Look Together

So you think that there is nothing on your resumé that anyone in the entertainment field would be interested in. That's where you are probably wrong. There's likely to be a lot on your resumé that will be interesting to a prospective internship coordinator. It's all in the way you look at it.

You need to understand the purpose of a resumé in order to create an effective one. This is a place where many prospective interns get stuck.

First, you need to have a handle on your skills and abilities. Be realistic. If you know you are good at something, that's fine to include it on your resumé. But if your skills are weak in one particular area, it's better not to list it. Your resumé is an advertising piece for you and you don't want it to be misleading in terms of what you have to offer.

Whether you are going for an internship or a paid job, you need to market yourself. Think of yourself as you would any other product that you might consider buying.

Let's try it with an example. If you were a soda, what you do is quench people's thirst and what I can expect as a person ready to buy the soda, is that I will enjoy the taste and maybe feel energized at the same time. If you were preparing an advertising campaign for the soda, you would want to market those selling points.

So now apply the same concepts to yourself. Focus on what you can do well. If you are good at production, you might market yourself as "competent and creative with digital editing". Next, describe how that translates into benefits for the company you would like to intern with. Perhaps you would say something like "with the ability to edit commercials, shows, PSAs, and other production elements".

Making a simple chart as you work all of this out will help you when you start creating your resumé, and also as you prepare your talking points for an interview later on in the application process.

Your chart could look something like this:

| What I Can Do (Skill) | How Could It Be Used at an Internship |
| --- | --- |
| Use ProTools | Edit commercials, show clips, production |
| Use Avid (or other video editing software) | Edit video footage for news, videos, films |
| Write news | Write stories for Radio/TV news, blogs, websites |
| Use social media | Handle social media accounts for internship site or for individual personalities |
| Entertain crowds | Work on station street teams for remote broadcasts and personal appearances for talent |

Keep on adding the skills you are proficient in and how you can put those skills to use at your internship. These will be "selling" points when you talk about why you are an excellent candidate for the position.

With that done, it's time to start putting together your resumé and cover letter, in that order. Think of this as you would a book. If you wanted to read a book but didn't know which book you wanted, you might check out each book's table of contents until you found one that sounded interesting. You would then read the book to get the details.

A good resumé is like a table of contents to your life, as it relates to work and education. It's a list of where you've worked, gone to school, and what you did and accomplished while you were there. And you want to make it a list, not a story. No one has time to go through a lot of information, especially at this beginning stage of the interaction. Tell too much on the resumé and you have no reason for the person to read the book . . . or in your case, meet you for an interview. Don't blow your chance to charm them in person.

Before we consider content, let's talk about presentation. If something doesn't look good, we often tend to think that it isn't going to be good either. A resumé that is not formatted properly or is messy or hard to read gives a bad first impression and may not even be looked at, except as it gets tossed in the trash. Your resumé represents you, so you need to be sure that your resumé looks good.

There are plenty of good websites out there to help you with creating a proper resumé. But generally these are pretty generic and you're going after an internship in the entertainment industry. Don't miss out on the chance to show some creativity with your resumé.

You can do this in any number of ways, but be careful not to get carried away. Stay away from being too cute or too wild. It may not have the desired effect. Cartoon characters, graphics, thoughtful sayings or pictures of tools used in the trade like a microphone or a movie camera really don't belong on your resumé. You can still show creativity while keeping the look professional and business-like.

Think about using a variety of font sizes but do stick with the same font throughout your resumé. Keep your resumé to one page and your font size to at least 12 point. You don't want someone to have to use a magnifying glass to read it. Set up the sections so they are easy to distinguish from one another and bold your headings to help organize them.

You might consider using a simple border on your resumé as well, shading your contact information or using a mix of bold and un-bolded text. A good-looking resumé gives the immediate impression of someone who is organized, mature and professional . . . even before it's read.

There are some examples of format and other ideas at the end of the chapter.

If you are actually going to send or deliver the resumé and cover letter as a hard copy as opposed to emailing it, think about the paper you are going to have it printed on. Use a quality paper, not copy paper. Use something with more stability to it . . . like a lighter weight card stock. Selecting a little heavier paper stock will also help your resumé stay looking good as it is shifted from pile to pile on a desk. You won't want to fold this heavier paper to put it in a standard envelope, so this gives you a reason to send it in a 9 × 12 flat envelope. When you mix it with all the standard sized envelopes, it's just another way to stand out from the crowd and get noticed in that pile of mail.

And consider using a colored paper and envelopes. Using a colored paper stock makes it easy for your resumé to be spotted in a stack of hundreds of others. Stay away from neon brights, but a light blue or green will make your resumé easy to locate in the stack of white papers that usually end up on a person's desk. It also says that you know how to get attention and are basically not the same as everyone else.

No matter how you design your resumé, there are certain things that it must include.

First is your contact information. It belongs right at the top of your resumé. You want to make it easy for a prospective internship coordinator to reach you. Center your information and make the font slightly bigger than the one you are using in the body of your resumé. You may want to make it bold as well. Put your name, first and last, complete address, phone number . . . don't forget your area code . . . and your email address.

Here is where many students get into trouble without even realizing it. Right now, think of what the outgoing message on your voicemail says. Messages that start with something like "Yo" or "Hey" or play 30 seconds of your favorite song are not going to give a potential internship employer the impression that you want to give. Now is the time to change that message to something more professional. Make it simple. Your message might be scripted like this:

> "Hi, This is (your name) and I'm not available to take your call right now. Please leave your name and telephone number along with a brief message and I will call you back just as soon as possible."

It doesn't have to be any more than that. Record and listen to it back to make sure that you are speaking clearly. But do keep the personality in it. After all, we are talking about the entertainment business here.

And while we're at it, take a look at your email address. Most of us have some "interesting" email addresses just for fun, but again, think about what yours says about you. SexiestGuyIn TheWorld@email.com or SuperHotChick@email.com might be fun, but they likely won't get the response you want from the person you want to hire you. A more professional email using just your name is a much better choice for use on your resumé.

Going back to our book analogy, your resumé is like the table of contents in that book. It gives an overview of the topics that will be covered. That's exactly what your resumé should do.

Many people choose to start their resumé with a short statement (objective) about what they want to do. If you do this, keep it general. Don't tailor your objective to the specific company where you plan to send the resumé. It should pertain to what you want to do overall, right now, career-wise . . . not your ultimate dream job where you're running the network or walking on the red carpet. Those are long term goals and not something that a person considering you for an internship needs to know at this point.

You want the employer to see that you have some direction in mind, but that you are also realistic about where you are at the moment, so make your objective something about getting your foot in the door or getting your first experience at a real studio/station/company, etc.

A big danger with this step is to over value your potential contribution. You want your objective statement to explain to the person reading your resumé why they received it and what you are hoping will happen. You also want to make it clear that while you have skills already, you are not a "know-it-all" and want to learn. Remember, your resumé is being read by someone who is already successful in the business and you are just getting started. It's important to blow your own horn, just not too loudly. You are not being hired as an intern to fix problems at the station or studio or to put it on the right track. Keep it simple and reflective of where you are at the moment in your pursuit of your career.

Consider something like this:

> "I am interested in an internship where I can use and expand my current skills and learn new ones."

It's simple and tells the reader that you already know some things, but also that you do not think you know everything and want to improve and learn.

What comes next on your resumé depends on what you have been doing. If you've been working at the campus radio or television station, then start with your experience section. If you have won any student awards for your work in college, start with an awards section. If your class work constitutes your related experience, then start with education. A list of your skills is also a great place to start. Whatever you decide, start with the section that contains your most relative and impressive entertainment-related experience. You want this information to be noticed most of all, so don't let it get buried further down the page. You've probably heard the phrase "save the best for last". When it comes to resumés, put your best close to the top.

Keep in mind the idea of a book index. You don't want to go into much detail on any of your resumé entries. Treat this like a list of possible things to talk about in the interview. That's where you can explain exactly what kind of piece won the award or what a customer specialist does.

In our example, let's start with education, college first. What is your education goal; a degree, certificate? In what? And what areas pertaining to that have you studied? This is a quick overview for the employer of what you know.

List the name of your school. Spell it out. You might call it by an acronym, but not everyone will know what those initials mean, so write out the entire name of the college. Include the city and state and the month and year that you started. If you're still attending, you would add "to present". If you have already graduated, list the month and year that you were awarded your certificate or degree.

Now give the reader an idea of what that degree or certificate covered. Stay away from the formal names of your classes. Colleges tend to give classes long and often confusing names that don't really give much of a clue as to what was covered in the class. Just list them by topic. I like the phrase 'Coursework included work in . . .' This will provide excellent opportunities during your interview for you to expand on what you know and what you can do.

If you went to an additional college, list it next in exactly the same way.

Depending on your age and experience you might list your high school information. If you decide to and were involved in activities in addition to your classes, list those things. It might be something in athletics, student government, clubs or any honors that you earned. No, the reader of your resumé won't be that fascinated that you were treasurer of the French Club, but what those extra-curricular activities show is that you can multi-task and that you do more than just what's required to get by. And who knows, the person who will be interviewing you might have been in French Club too back in their high school days and now you two have something in common. It all counts.

Let's take experience next . . . if you have it. If you don't have any entertainment-related experience, it's ok. Just leave this section out. You'll have plenty of other information to put on your resumé. But remember, it's very important to get involved in anything on your campus that has to do with the area of entertainment that you want to go into so you will have something to go in this section. This is where the pay-off for all that hard work comes in.

If you worked at the college radio or TV station or the campus theater in any capacity, were an officer in any related clubs on campus or hosted, voiced, wrote, directed, or produced any programs or plays for the school or even as a class project, this is where you list it. You probably weren't paid for any of this, but you don't need to make a point of that on your resumé. What matters is that you did the work and gained the experience.

See, you're not as much of a beginner as you thought you were when you started.

Your work history section follows and it's not going to be a problem if your jobs just consisted of flipping burgers or ringing up sales. This is another place where you can show that you really do know how to balance more than one thing (school and work) at the same time and do it successfully. You're in great shape if you've kept some of those jobs for more than just a few months. It shows you can commit to something . . . and that's especially impressive if it's one of those mundane minimum wage jobs! That looks good to an employer and keep in mind that the person who will be interviewing you *is* an employer, even if you are just applying for an internship.

While working at the campus book store or the local burger restaurant may not seem very relevant or even interesting, there are some components to jobs like these that can be important. Working and going to school at the same time is not easy. The fact that you did both shows a commitment to your career goals and is a sign of maturity. The fact that you kept that job six months or more proves that you must have been doing a good job. All of these are qualities that anyone considering working with you will consider important. So keep those jobs on your resumé, as unrelated to the entertainment industry as they are.

Many people also like to detail the duties that go with each job listed on their resumé. That's fine, but you don't have to go into much, if any, detail about jobs that the average person is familiar with. If you waitressed, there is no need to go into details such as "took people's orders and delivered their food to their table when it was ready." We all know that is what a waitress does and with your resumé confined to just one page, you can't afford to waste the space. List the job title and move on.

If you did something at the job that is above the average, such as supervised and trained the waitress staff, that is something that would have some value in listing with the corresponding position.

You'll also want to include a skills section. Here's the big finale where you detail all the *other* great things that you bring to the table. List things like your ability to read and write any languages other than English, list all the computer skills you have (what programs you know and can handle competently) and most of all, list any professional software or hardware that you are familiar with such as editing, programming or production programs. When it comes to skills, the easiest way to list them is with bullet points.

If you are lucky enough to be going to a college that uses the same technologies as those that are being used in the industry, and you've taken the opportunity to learn them, make that known. List these as well in this skills section and be sure to use the commercial names and that they are spelled right. For example, a very common mistake students make is in listing the editing software ProTools. That's right, there is no space between the 'Pro' and the 'Tools' and the 'T' is capitalized. If you want a potential employer to believe you know how to use it, you should know how to spell it.

This section can be very important. Most employers don't expect a college student to even know about these programs, let alone be able to use them. So make sure to be thorough in this list. At the same time, only list programs and software that you are competent in at this moment. It can be very difficult and embarrassing to have to explain to your internship supervisor why you can't use something that you indicated on your resumé that you were proficient with.

This is also the section where you can get bonus points for being a maven of social media. Yes, Facebook, Twitter and the like are work-related skills. They're one of the biggest selling points right now. The ability to effectively use social media is highly prized at most companies and can turn out to be the key to getting your foot in the door.

List all the social media platforms that you use and are familiar with in your skills section. And you've likely heard it a million times already, make sure there is nothing on your social media that you don't want a prospective internship coordinator to see. Social media can make or break you as you begin to enter the industry.

Your resumé is part of the first impression you will be giving a prospective internship coordinator, so make sure it is neat and contains no misspelled or incorrect words. How you present yourself on your resumé can be translated into how you will do your work if you get the internship, so be careful, spellcheck and double check.

Finally, your cover letter. It should be short and to the point, but with enough information to convince the internship coordinator to take a look at your resumé. Use it to introduce yourself and state that you are interested in an internship with that company, studio, etc. Then come up with a couple of interesting facts about you that will make them want to know more.

Make sure to put your contact information on your cover letter. It doesn't matter if it's also on your resumé. The two might become separated. Very few people are going to search through everything on their desk to find both pieces and match them up. You want to get a response, so make it easy for that to happen by including your complete contact information on everything.

There are several good examples of resumés and cover letters on the next few pages.

**Mailed Cover Letter Example (sent to someone you have not spoken to yet)**


Dear (name of person),

I am very interested in doing my college internship with your company. I spoke to (here is where you put the name of the receptionist or secretary that you talked with) who said you were the person in charge of those positions.

My resumé is attached. You'll see that I have spent two semesters anchoring the college station's TV newscasts and that I am proficient at using ProTools for editing and production (list a couple of your accomplishments and one or two of your skills).

I look forward to meeting with you to talk about this possibility. I can be reached at (phone number) or by email at (email address).

Thank-you,

Your Name

**Email Cover Letter Example (sent to someone you have already spoken to)**

Dear (name of person),

Thank you for taking time to talk with me today. I am very interested in doing my college internship with your company.

My resumé is attached. As I mentioned on the phone, I've spent two semesters anchoring the college station's TV newscasts and that I am proficient at using ProTools for editing and production.

(Recap a couple of the accomplishments and skills that you mentioned on the phone. If you didn't talk about any, then your paragraph could read:)

I am looking forward to coming in to talk with you more about this possibility. I can be reached at (phone number) or by email at (email address).

Thank-you,

Your Name

**Mailed Cover Letter Example (sent to someone you have already spoken to)**

Dear (name of person),

Thank you for taking time to talk with me today. I am very interested in doing my college internship with your company.

My resumé is enclosed. As I mentioned on the phone, I've spent two semesters anchoring the college station's TV newscasts and that I am proficient at using ProTools for editing and production.

(Recap a couple of the accomplishments and skills that you mentioned on the phone. If you didn't talk about any, then your paragraph could read:)

As I mentioned on the phone, I've spent two semesters anchoring the college stations TV newscasts and that I am proficient at using ProTools for editing and production.

I am looking forward to coming in to talk with you more about this possibility. I can be reached at (phone number) or by email at (email address).

Thank-you,

Your Name

**Mailed Cover Letter Example (sent to someone you have not spoken to yet)**

Dear (name of person),

I am very interested in doing my college internship with your company. I spoke to (here is where you put the name of the receptionist or secretary that you talked with) who said you were the person in charge of those positions.

My resumé is attached. You'll see that I have spent two semesters anchoring the college station's TV newscasts and that I am proficient at using ProTools for editing and production (list a couple of your accomplishments and one or two of your skills).

I look forward to meeting with you to talk about this possibility. I can be reached at (phone number) or by email at (email address).

Thank-you,

Your Name

## Resumé Example #1

**Your Name**
Your address, city, state, zip code
Your phone number
Your email address

_____ **Profile** _____

Motivated radio/TV/film (pick one or change) student is ready to launch into the Entertainment Industry. Looking for an internship where I can use what I already know and learn more from professionals in the business.

_____ **Education** _____

Bachelor of Arts—Radio TV Broadcasting June 2016
Name of College, City, State

Coursework included:
Audio Production, Video Production, Editing, Commercial Voicing, Communication Law, Story Boarding, Lighting On-Set Direction

_____ **Related Work Experience** _____

XYZ Production Studio October 2015–present
City, State
• List a variety of the tasks you handled
• Include only those that are of a professional nature
• Do not include any gopher jobs such as getting coffee

K-WWW Radio November 2014–October 2015
City, State
• task
• task
• task
List any additional jobs that relate to your career choice.

_____ **Additional Work Experience** _____

• Fast Food Restaurant, City, State, Job Title, Date started to date left
• List more of the same

_____ **Skills** _____

• ProTools (Use bullet points to list the industry-related computer programs and hardware that you know how to use)
• Include all your social media skills as well

## Resumé Example #2

**Your Name**
Your address, city, state, zip code
Your phone number
Your email address
Your website if you have one

Motivated radio/TV/film (pick one or change) student is ready to launch into the Entertainment Industry. Looking for an internship where I can use what I already know and learn more from professionals in the business.

### QUALIFICATIONS
- Pro Tools (Use bullet points to list the industry-related computer programs and hardware that you know how to use)
  - Include all your social media skills as well

### PROFESSIONAL EXPERIENCE
XYZ Production Studio October 2015–present
City, State
List a variety of the tasks you handled
Include only those that are of a professional nature
Do not include any gopher jobs such as getting coffee

K-WWW Radio November 2015–October 2015
City, State
List any additional jobs that relate to your career choice.

### WORK HISTORY
- Fast Food Restaurant, City, State Job Title Date started to date left
  - List more of the same

### EDUCATION
Bachelor of Arts—Radio TV Broadcasting June 2016
College of California, City, State

Coursework included:
Audio Production, Video Production, Editing, Commercial Voicing,
Communication Law, Story Boarding, Lighting On-Set Direction

### AWARDS/ACHIEVEMENTS
Use bullet points to list awards, scholarships, Honor Society memberships, committees you served on and anything else that will make you and your work stand out.

## Resumé Example #3

# YOUR NAME

**Your address, city, state, zip code**
**Your phone number**
**Your email address**
**Your website if you have one**

Motivated Radio/TV/Film (pick one or change) student is ready to launch into the Entertainment Industry. Looking for an internship where I can use what I already know and learn more from professionals in the business.

**EDUCATION:**
Name of College, City, State                                    Year Graduated
Degree earned

Course work included: Audio and Video Production, Audio and Video Editing, Commercial Voicing, Communication Law, Story Boarding, Lighting, On-Set Direction

**RELATED WORK EXPERIENCE:**
XYZ Production Studio, City, State                    Date started to date left
List a variety of the tasks you handled. Include only those that were of a professional nature. Do not include any gopher jobs such as getting coffee

K-WWW Radio, City State                                Date started to date left
List important tasks

List any other jobs you have held that relate to your career choice

**WORK HISTORY**
Fast Food Restaurant, City, State      Job Title            Date started to date left
List more of the same

**SKILLS**
Use bullet points to list the industry-related computer programs and hardware that you know how to use. Include all your social media skills as well

**AWARDS AND ACHIEVEMENTS**
Use bullet points to list awards, scholarships, Honor Society memberships, committees you served on and anything else that will make you and your work stand out.

The way you deliver your cover letter and resumé is another area in which you can get creative. Often, resumés are sent as email attachments leaving your cover letter to essentially be the email itself. In this case, the design of the resumé becomes even more important as it is the only thing that the prospective employer will really see.

If you've already created a website for yourself, you can put the information from your resumé on your site and then direct the employer over to it with a link in your email. A website gives you another chance to show your creativity but it is also the mark of a professional and will make you look even more ready to enter the industry.

You can also put your audio and/or video demos, if you have them on your site. While they may not be required by the person hiring interns at the company, having them available can't hurt and just gives that person a chance to see more of what you have to offer.

If you are using a link to direct someone to your website, it is still a good idea to also attach a copy of your resumé to your email. That way, they will have it as a separate piece that they can print out if they need or want to.

Mailing your materials or dropping them by the company can give you some interesting advantages . . . and in the case of one example, some disadvantages.

In an effort to get noticed, one person I know sent their resumé in an envelope that also contained a large quantity of sparkly pieces of glitter. They wanted to get the recipient's attention and show that they were not the ordinary internship candidate. The idea though backfired when the glitter all came out with the resumé, getting all over the person and their desk and creating a huge mess. Think your ideas through *very* carefully.

Another approach was nothing short of brilliant. Instead of an envelope, the resumé was delivered in a box. Boxes are interesting because they hold an air of intrigue and they certainly stand out when most business mail comes in envelopes. Boxes are also rarely opened by anyone other than the person to whom they are addressed, so your materials are likely not going to get stuck with a secretary or an assistant.

When the box was opened, inside was the hand from a mannequin and it was holding a cassette tape of the person's demo. There was also a string hanging from the mannequin's thumb that read "Let Me Give You a Hand".

Now, all groans aside, was there any way that the person who got this could keep themselves from running into a studio and listening to that tape? Absolutely not! Their curiosity was peaked by the presentation. And it certainly showed that the sender was creative. Of course, no one uses cassettes anymore, but the idea could easily work with a CD or a thumb drive. Or even with the resumé itself.

Granted, both of those are rather extreme examples, but the idea is to stand out. You just want to make sure to think your ideas through to their conclusions so you spot any potential pitfalls before they happen (like with the glitter that the person is probably still cleaning up!)

Now that you've got your materials looking good, let's talk about how you plan to look. Business experts say you only have seven seconds to make a good visual impression. That means that first impression is key.

Our brains are hardwired from long ago to make immediate decisions about the people we meet. In many ways, it's not even a conscious process. But once those decisions are made, they might as well be carved in stone.

One nice thing about the entertainment industry is that it tends to be pretty casual. That doesn't mean jeans and flip-flops are ok but it doesn't necessarily mean a suit and tie in most cases either. You want your appearance to enhance your personal brand and be appropriate for the area of the industry that you are targeting. It's ok to show your own unique style, but make sure that what you wear is suitable for the workplace. The same goes for your hair, make-up (if you wear it) and jewelry. You want the focus to be on you, not on what you are wearing. Keep it simple and tasteful.

An important key is to look like you belong in the workplace you are applying to. You can do a lot of your research online. Check out company websites and Facebook pages to get an idea of what people working at the company are wearing. A good rule of thumb is to then step it up a notch for your interview. A word of warning though! Even if you see a lot of people wearing jeans, and you likely will, jeans are never a good choice for an interview. Even very expensive jeans just have too much of a casual appearance to make them appropriate for this first meeting.

This is the time that you want to make an investment in some business clothing. Men should consider wearing a nice pair of pants or khakis and a polo shirt, button-down shirt or a sweater. Shirts should be tucked in and worn with a belt. You could also opt for a sport coat or jacket. Tennis shoes, sneakers or sandals are out. In the majority of cases, forget the tie, but don't forget the black or dark socks. You don't want a flash of white sock showing if you cross your legs.

Women have more options. You don't necessarily have to wear a dress, but if you do, make sure that it is not too short or too revealing. If you're interviewing at a more conservative company, you likely should wear pantyhose for a more professional look. Nice pants are another good alternative with a matching or coordinated jacket. Wear a shirt, blouse or sweater, but make sure it's not cut too low. If you think it might be, don't wear it. As for shoes, wear flats or low to medium heels so you'll be able to walk comfortably in them.

The bottom line is that you want to be comfortable and look good. Plan your outfit ahead of time so you make sure everything works before the day of your interview and you have time to correct what doesn't.

Another wise investment is in business cards or more accurately calling cards. They are a standard in every type of business and allow you to quickly and easily give someone your contact information. Without cards, you usually end up trying to find something to write on and that little scrap of paper gets easily lost.

While you won't have a company listed on your card, you can put your name, your skill sets and your phone, email and social media contact information which could look like this:

Your business card is also another opportunity to show off your style, brand and creativity. And it doesn't have to cost a lot. There are a number of great websites that offer you the chance to create your own card online and are surprisingly inexpensive. They generally have hundreds of preset templates and offer fonts, borders, graphics, and a chance to upload your own logo and such.

Most of these sites also offer templates tailored to different industries. Just like you did on your resumé, it really is a good idea to stay away from ones that feature things like movie reels, cameras or microphones. That's what everyone else is going to do and part of the key to being successful in any area of the entertainment industry is to avoid doing what everyone else is doing.

A glossy finish on a business card always looks classier and most of the time, if you pay a small additional fee you can eliminate the card company's website information from the backside of your design. Most people prefer to have the backsides blank so they can make notes on them.

There are some things that you should take to the interview with you. We'll talk more about these in a later chapter, but they should include a copy of your resumé and any demos or portfolios that show your skills and talent. Jamming them into a backpack or an overstuffed purse is not the best idea. Consider getting some sort of briefcase or use a large 9 x 12 inch envelope to carry your materials to the interview. You want to keep your hands free and don't want to be dropping things or scrambling to keep your materials together.

Finally, let's talk about the handshake. It's probably going to be how you are greeted and it's another part of that first impression. Your handshake should be solid and last only a few seconds. It's not a strength contest, but nobody wants to shake hands with a "limp fish" either. Smile and look the person in the eye as you shake hands. And if you are sitting down when you are introduced, stand up before you shake his or her hand.

You now have the tools to beat the competition and land your internship!

## POINTS TO REMEMBER

- Make your resumé no more than one page.
- Design your resumé so it is well organized and looks neat.
- Spellcheck!
- List only skills that you are competent in.
- Make sure your email and voicemail message sound professional.
- You only have seven seconds to make that all important first impression.
- Learn to shake hands properly.

# Chapter 3

# Preparing to Go For It!

- Where do You Look for an Internship
- What to Say When You Call

So you have everything together . . . your materials and your look. Now it's on to making contacts and setting up interviews. The first step is to figure out where you want to intern. Yes, where you *want* to intern.

Remember, this is your chance to get out into the real world for the first time and really see what goes on. So what would you like to see? What area do you feel your skills line up with best? Some students are 100 percent sure where they want to intern. For others, it's another chance to explore and gather information before making that final commitment to a career choice. There is no harm in doing several internships before you settle down on the part of the industry that you want to enter. While most students are eager to get that degree and get going, this is not a race and a little more preparation will likely make you just that more employable when the time comes to go for your first job.

There are a lot of great websites where companies list openings for interns and they are certainly worth checking out. Do a Google search for "Entertainment Internships" and you will come up with plenty of them. But this may not be the best way to find an internship.

First, just think how many other people are likely seeing these listings as well. The more people that see them, the more people who apply, and the greater the competition is for getting that internship. It's also hard to tell how old these listings are. You may be pursuing an opening that has been filled for weeks or even months.

And finally, many of these sites charge a membership fee for you to be able to look through the listings. Even though the fees are generally small, if you pay at a number of sites, it adds up. And it's not necessary.

Again, think about where you *want* to intern. Think about the radio and TV stations in your area. Search the Internet for local production companies, cable stations, recording studios. No matter what area of the entertainment business you are considering going into, you should be able to find a company that deals with that area.

Just because you don't see a listing on one of the internship websites you might look at, that doesn't necessarily mean the company doesn't have an opening. Not every company, and in fact relatively few, actually take the time to list their available internships on these sites. If they do list them online at all, you're really more likely to find them on the company's own website. But again, whether or not you see a listing, that doesn't mean that interning at that company is not a possibility.

All of these companies are businesses, not secret entities. They need to attract customers, just like any other business does. So they list their phone numbers and addresses online, on Facebook, on 411. If it's a particular TV show that you want to do your internship with, watch the credits at the end of the show. If they move too fast, record them and slow them down. You will find the name of the production company behind that show. The same goes for movies, although you will likely find the name of the companies—and there are often several—during the opening credits. These are the companies that you will want to get in contact with. Not the channel or network that airs the show or the movie studio that released the film. You want to get to the company that is actually responsible for making the show or film.

Internships are also listed on sites such as Craig's List. While many of the companies listed on such sites are solid businesses, there have been instances where they were not. Students have reported getting involved with "fly-by-night" companies that are there one day and the next time the student shows up for work, the company is closed or even totally gone. Other students have been promised jobs upon completion of the internship, prompting them to work enormous amounts of hours to secure a position that never materializes and likely never existed at all.

If you are considering pursuing an internship that you see on such a site, do your "due diligence" and really check it out. Do an Internet search for any information about the company or call the local union that would cover the type of work that the company does and ask if they have any information on the organization or if they've even heard of it. The entertainment industry is pretty close-knit and everyone seems to know everyone else, so it shouldn't be hard to determine if the company is legitimate with just a few calls. You want to make sure that you are working for a reputable company, not just for the experience, but for your own safety as well.

While there are certainly companies where you could do your internship locally in your area, some students consider moving to get to a larger market and a larger company. Depending on what part of the country you live in, this might make good sense, but you need to do some serious thinking before committing to this plan. The majority of internships remember, are unpaid and if they are paid, it's often at minimum wage and not much more. If you are considering moving away from home to do your internship, your earning potential is going to be quite limited. Make sure you can afford to live on your own and support yourself during your internship before you start making the contacts and getting the ball rolling. Paid internship also usually requires you to work a 40-hour week, so there's not much time to take on a second paying job to help make ends meet.

Whether you find your internship close to home or decide to move . . . in this case bigger is not always better. Here are some things you need to consider. Which do you prize higher . . . a big name company, production or show or the chance to do more actual hands-on work? In some cases, you can get both from the same internship, but not always.

Bigger companies have constraints such as union prohibitions on non-union people, which at this point you probably are. It means that certain types of work can only be done by someone who is in the appropriate union. Allowing a non-union person to do the work would be union violation and could get the company hit with a large fine. At a company like this, you are going to find yourself doing a lot of watching as opposed to actual doing. And at the larger companies there is more at stake, so they are often not too keen on turning it over to an intern with limited actual experience.

Smaller companies may not deal with such constraints. Many are not in unions or are not covered by as many unions, so there are fewer areas where interns are kept from doing substantive work. They also generally have fewer employees overall and often actually rely on well-qualified interns to get certain jobs done.

While the name of the company might not bring as much punch to your resumé, you actually may come out of the internship with more marketable skills, which when it comes down to it, are what are going to help you most in your career.

There are also the prohibitions spelled out by the Fair Labor Standards Act that we discussed in Chapter One. These will likely also have some impact on what you are allowed to do at your internship.

No matter how large or small the company you land an internship with is, your main focus has got to be on learning. If a company takes on an intern, it is part of their responsibility to make sure that the intern gets a chance to learn and is legally bound to make sure that those opportunities are made available.

Whatever companies you decide to pursue as possible internship opportunities, do your homework before you start making contact. Find out everything that you can about the company. Things like what projects they have in the works, how successful previous projects were, the names of the show hosts. You want to have this information in your head because you may be asked about some of it by the person who hires the interns.

A former student of mine lost a great internship because he was not able to name at least two of the station's DJs. To make it worse, while he could name one of them, he made up a name for the second one. Double mistake. He compounded not having a piece of information by trying to fake it and he did it in front of someone who would obviously know he was faking! If you don't know something, it will be far less damaging to simply admit that you don't have the answer. But doing your research and then reviewing your information before making any calls or going to an interview will help ensure that you are ready for anything.

The bottom line in starting your search for an internship is to find a company where you would like to intern, get a contact phone number and make the call!

When you start this part of the process, it's a good idea to keep track of your progress. You want to keep a list that shows the name of each company you call, the date you call and what happens during the call. This way you'll be able to do proper follow-up later. It's also important to make a note of the names of the people you talk to. That way if you need to call back, you can ask for that same person and not have to start the process all over again with someone new.

Let's talk a little bit more about asking and remembering people's names. Studies have shown that people find value and self-worth from hearing their own names. People who know us use our names. It's a sign of familiarity. Strangers don't use our names because they don't know us. While you won't really "know" the person on the other end of the line when you start making a call, using their name creates a feeling that the two of you are acquainted. It can have an impact on how willing they are to help you.

You probably will first talk to a secretary or receptionist. This is a very important person. They can get you in touch with the person you need to talk to. Be courteous and remember, they probably have a number of lines going at once, so you don't want to waste their time. Get to the point quickly. Your initial conversation might go something like this:

> "Hi, I'm (name) and I am a film/broadcasting/production, etc. student at (school name). I was wondering who at your company handles internships."

Make a note of the name of the person who you are told deals with internships and if it's a hard name to understand or pronounce, ask the secretary or receptionist to say it again and to spell it. And thank them at the end of the call . . . by name.

That's it. It really is that simple.

Chances are you will either be connected to that person or sent to their voicemail. Be ready for either one. This is your chance to make a first impression, so you want to be prepared and know what to say.

If the person answers, you might say something like (and this is where having the name of the secretary or receptionist can be really important):

"Hi (name of person), Susan told me that you were the person who handles internships. My name is (name) and I'm a student at (school name). I'm very interested in interning with your company."

Did you catch what happened? By knowing the name of the secretary or receptionist who forwarded you, you were able to use it in your introduction. You're not just an unknown now; you have a referral from that person.

Keep your pen handy. The person you are talking to will probably now give you instructions on how that company handles applications for internships. You may be told to email your resumé and cover letter. If you are, make sure to repeat back the email address so that you are sure that you get it right.

You might also be asked to tell a little bit about yourself. Get this together ahead of time so you are not caught off-guard. The person is not asking for information such as where you were born or what your favorite hobbies are. They are looking for information to show them why they should be interested in you.

This can be a turning point for you. Remember, they are probably talking to a lot of people. Tell them something that will make them remember you. Think of accomplishments you have had related to the entertainment field. Any college work that really made you look good or that was unique. Tell them why you want to get in the field, what attracts you? The most everyone else is going to give them is a mini-bio. You want to give them something to remember.

It's also possible that you will be invited in for an interview. This can happen, even if the person has not seen your resumé yet. Perhaps they would rather meet candidates in person and go over the resumé face-to-face or you might have done such a great job in the initial phone call that they simply would like to meet you in person.

The reason doesn't really matter. What matters is that you are one step closer to getting the internship you want. If the person asks you when you want to come in, a great response would be "Whatever works best for you will be fine for me."

If they ask you to name a time and date, select something within the next day or so. You want to get the meeting as close to the phone call as you can so they will remember why they invited you in.

Make your calendar open when it comes to scheduling. If you have to go back and forth to find a time that works, it gives the appearance that you may be too busy to actually commit to an internship. It also can convey the message that the internship doesn't really matter enough to you to make an effort to find a time to fit the interview in.

## POINTS TO REMEMBER

- If there is a company or studio where you would like to do your internship, give them a call. Not every company with open internships advertises.
- Smaller companies may give you more "hands-on" experience.
- Keep good notes when you start making calls to set up interviews. The information will come in handy when you start making follow-up calls.
- Think about what you want to say before you make a call. Write down some bullet points so you don't forget important topics or points.

# Part 2

# Getting the Internship

# Chapter 4

# The Interview

- Interrogation vs. Conversation
- How to Answer Questions While Telling Your Story
- The All-Time Dreaded Questions

Getting an interview is a big step. While you haven't got the internship yet, you at least have said, written, or done something that has gotten the person hiring for it interested in you. Now you want to build on that.

The day of the interview review the notes you made when you initially researched the company. Check online for any additional news about the company or the people who work there. Also check for any important news about the area of the entertainment field that the company you will be interviewing with is in. You will want to be able to talk intelligently about what is going on if there is.

You know you only have a couple of seconds to make that first impression and you will be making a first impression several times on the day of the interview.

First and foremost, be on time! In fact, be five to ten minutes early for your interview. Planning to be a bit early ensures that you will not be late because of traffic or other issues and it also gives you some time to relax, collect your thoughts and get your materials together before you sit down to talk.

The person you will meet first is probably the secretary or receptionist. This might be the person you initially spoke to on the phone, so review your notes before you go in so that you remember that person's name. If their name is not displayed on a plaque on their desk, once you introduce yourself and let them know who you have an appointment with, ask their name. If it is the same person, make sure you thank them for getting you to the right person when you initially called.

Now comes an opportunity that many students don't recognize. If the secretary or receptionist is not busy and seems friendly, it's a chance to not only get some additional information on the company that you might be able to use in the interview, but also to make a good impression on him or her. You can ask how long they have worked for the company and what they like most about it. If the person is busy handling calls or dealing with other employees, then don't interrupt and simply wait to be called for your appointment.

This is absolutely not the time to sit and play games on your phone or call a friend and tell them where you are. You would be surprised how many employers will check in with the secretary or receptionist to see how an internship or job candidate behaved while waiting for their appointment. This can be a "make-or-break" opportunity for you, so keep it professional and friendly and you will score some points before the interview ever starts.

That brings up an interesting question. When does the interview start? The correct answer is that it starts the moment you open the door to the office, studio, or station.

A few years ago, a student of mine was the prime candidate for an internship at a big Los Angeles station. He really did have the internship . . . as I like to say "it was his to lose."

The person he was meeting with came out to the reception area to take him back to her office. On the way there, she asked him how the drive getting to the station had been, noting that he had come from about 50 miles away. His response: "Wow, I don't know how people make that drive every day. It took forever."

He succeeded in losing the internship right then and there. If he felt that way about the drive already, it led the person interviewing him to feel that he might not stick with the position very long since the internship would require him to make the same drive at least a couple of times a week. A much better response, even if the drive had been horrible, would have been "Not that bad." Keep in mind that you want to keep things on a positive level during your entire interview experience.

But wait, had the interview actually started? That's what my student questioned afterwards, crying "Foul" . . . and noting the conversation was only in the hallway. He felt nothing he said should have counted until he was seated in the office of the person he was meeting with. Wrong. Never forget that the interview starts when you walk in the door and that everything you say and do can have an effect on whether or not you get the internship, or down the road a bit, the job.

The main event is of course the interview itself. There are actually two different kinds of interview. The first is the traditional interview with the person who does the hiring. But there is also the group interview. Many companies do this when they are looking at interns because it takes less time than doing one-on-one interviews. Most people do not like group interviews, but you have to learn to cope with them just the same.

Group interviews are interesting and present some very important psychological dynamics. There are generally four or five intern candidates and one interviewer. Each candidate starts by saying something about themselves. The majority of them are going to do the mini-bio consisting of where they were born, where they went to school, etc. As we talked about earlier, you can stand out right from the beginning of the interview by saying something interesting about yourself.

The group interview automatically is somewhat of a competition. Each person is trying to prove to the interviewer that they are the best person for the job. Often they accidently, or maybe on purpose, start trying to out do each other. You can stand out by not falling into that trap.

The interviewer may ask each candidate the same question in a sort of round-robin fashion. Or they may ask questions of each individual at random. Either way, focus on what you want to say and basically ignore what anyone else has said or answered.

It's also important not to physically react if another candidate gives an answer that you think is off-the-mark. You don't want to shake your head, roll your eyes, or in any way show what you are thinking. It is very unprofessional and it can hurt you. Most group interviewers make a point of watching for such reactions.

On the other hand, if another candidate makes a good point, it is totally acceptable to indicate your agreement or support of it with a smile or a nod of your head. Doing that shows the interviewer that you are mature enough and confident enough not to be threatened when a person you are actually in competition with does well.

One odd thing that often happens in a group interview is that the most qualified candidate will "dumb" down his or her answers and responses in an unconscious effort, it seems, to not show up the other people being interviewed. While that is considerate, it is contrary to your mission of winning the internship.

Don't worry about showing anyone up. Just answer the questions to the best of your ability.

Whether you are involved in a group interview or a one-on-one, be yourself, relax, and smile. Let the interviewer see you as a person. They're going to be trying to decide if you are a good fit for the company, even if this interview is only for an internship and not a job. You are still going to be in the building and involved with employees at the company so it's important that it looks like you can be an effective part of the team.

During the initial phone conversation you may have been asked to tell the interviewer something about yourself. Be prepared for the same request to open the "in-person" interview.

Remember, they're not asking what city you were born in, unless it is bizarre or exotic, or where you went to elementary school, or any other mundane biographical information about you. They are looking for something interesting about you; something that will reveal your true personality.

If you are meeting with someone other than the person you spoke to on the phone, then you can use the same story you used on the phone. If it is the same person, then you are going to have to come up with a new one, so work on this ahead of time.

Here's another reason you took notes during the first phone call and all the calls after that— you can keep the people straight. How embarrassing would it be to tell your interesting story again in person to the same person you already told it to on the phone. Keeping good notes on people's names and reviewing them before your interview will help keep you from making this kind of a mistake.

It's really valuable to consider the difference between an interview and an interrogation. In an interrogation, one person asks the questions and the other one answers them. It's stiff and sterile and usually makes the person doing the answering uncomfortable. A conversation is much more enjoyable . . . for both parties. Don't be afraid to make comments on things the interviewer says and to ask questions. You will likely have a lot of those and you want to get the answers while you have the chance.

Such questions might include information on what kind of tasks you will be doing during the internship, what days and hours they would need you, and whether they consider hiring interns when their internships are over.

This has to work both ways. Not only does the company have to feel that you're the right person for the internship, you have to determine if the internship is right for you. You can't do that without information. So don't be afraid to ask questions. While it might seem cool to be working at a big company with great name recognition among your peers, the focus of your internship should be in making contacts, learning how to navigate the industry, enhancing your skills and learning new ones.

If you find out that the internship that you are interviewing for will only give you the opportunity to be a gopher (as in go for this . . . go for that), you need to let the interviewer know that while you are willing to do those things . . . that you understand everyone needs to pay their dues . . . you are also looking for an internship that will also enhance what you have already learned in your college courses. If this is not what this particular internship involves, then you need to respectfully decline it right there at the interview.

If something is said that you don't understand, then ask for a clarification. No one expects you to understand everything at this point. If you did, you would probably be going for a job and not an internship. It is much better to ask and understand an answer than to assume you get it and then down the road realize that your interpretation was incorrect.

An internship student of mine once interviewed for a position with one of the top stations in the Los Angeles market on the number one show in the city. To make it even better, it was a paid internship. Only minimum wage, but money just the same.

During the interview, she asked what some of her tasks would be. She was told very clearly that primarily she would be getting the on-air personality his coffee and sodas during the show and that she would be parking his car in the parking garage since he liked to get out right in front of the building. When she learned that there would be very little opportunity beyond that, she told the interviewer that she was looking for an internship that would allow her to really learn how a successful radio morning show was done and turned down the internship. She ended up getting her internship with another station that was also in the top five and it served as a launching pad for her now very successful career. So it pays to ask those questions.

There are some questions that everyone worries about being asked in an interview. Interestingly, in many cases, the interviewer isn't really interested in the answer itself, but more in what the answer shows them about the person.

Here are some of the most dreaded questions and some ideas on how to handle them:

> • **What do you consider to be your biggest strength and your biggest weakness?**
>
> It is somewhat of a trick question. Everyone has weaknesses, so you really can't say you don't have any. But you don't want to present a laundry list of items either that could scare someone off. What the interviewer is really looking for is someone who has a handle on their strengths and is also aware of their weaknesses.
>
> We're not talking about your technical skills here, but about your work habits.
>
> One that I've often used is "I'm a perfectionist with my work. And this can be a good and a bad thing. I want to do the best job possible, but sometimes I end up working too long on a project." It covers both aspects of the question, citing both a strength and a weakness. It's easier to get someone to do work a little faster on doing a great job than to get someone who is doing a poor or sloppy job to slow down and do better work.

- **Why do you want to be in the entertainment business?**

While it might be partially or even totally true, fame and fortune are not good answers to this question. In fact, they are exactly the kind of answers that the interviewer does not want to hear. They show greed and a rather poor understanding of how the business actually works. You would do better with answers that demonstrate that you already have ideas for projects or programs that you hope to someday create and launch.

Be prepared to explain why you think the ideas would be successful as well. Here's your chance to show you have a working understanding in a number of areas. You might compare your idea to a similar one that succeeded or talk about what's missing in a certain area of entertainment and how your project would fill that gap. Warning, make sure the company you're hoping to intern with does not work in that area and is not part of what you consider is missing.

- **What so far has been your favorite class in college and why?**

Obviously, this should be something in your major and it's a great opportunity for you to highlight an accomplishment or a project! Name the class, describe briefly what it covered, and then talk about the project that won you that award, or the skill that you mastered while doing it.

- **How do you handle controversy in the work-place?**

Watch your step here! The person asking the question likely wants to get an idea of how mature you are when it comes to dealing with difficult or stressful situations.

No business wants someone who will get into an open controversy but at the same time, controversial situations need to be resolved or they generally just get worse.

- **Where do you see yourself in five years?**

This is another of the universally dreaded interview questions. Since you are going for an internship, you can be a bit vague. The key here is to keep it realistic. Saying that you want to be the head of programming for a chain of radio stations or the C.E.O. of a major motion picture studio will make it sound like you have your head in the clouds. It's also a very poor idea to tell your interviewer that you would like to have their job. Before you laugh, believe me, it's happened.

Rather than answer the question "exactly", you can make a better impression by saying that in five years, you hope to have increased your skills in (list a number of areas that are applicable to your ultimate goal) and be on your way to reaching that goal.

- **What is the ultimate goal in your career?**

This is another time that it's actually ok to admit that you're not sure. If you are sure, then go ahead and talk about your plans. After all, the question did say "ultimate". But if you aren't ready to make this informal commitment, then consider an answer that demonstrates you understand that the entertainment industry can be full of surprises, especially with the continuing evolution of new technology, but also shows you have thought about your future. Go ahead and be a bit vague . . . something like "I know I want to work in directing. That might be in movies or television, but I'm also becoming very interested in projects that are going direct to the Internet." This type of answer also shows that you are keeping up with new developments in the business.

Hopefully you noticed that in most cases, the goal was to not only try to provide an answer to the question, but also to use the question to provide an opportunity to give more information.

When the interview is winding up, many interviewers will ask if you have any questions for them. Too many times, prospective interns say no. There is absolutely no way that everything you need and want to know has been covered in a half-hour long interview. There has to be at least one or two questions that you still have. Now is the time to ask them. Asking questions proves to the interviewer that you have been engaged in the interview and is a chance to show that you are knowledgeable about both the company and the industry.

Another way to go when asked if you have any questions, is to ask about the person who has been conducting the interview. Ask them about their background, how long have they been with the company, what do they like most about their job. Again, you are displaying curiosity that goes hand-in-hand with being interested and you are also acknowledging that your interviewer is a person as well.

Whether people want to admit it or not, they are their own favorite topic. Up until now, the interview has pretty much been all about you. By reversing the roles of interviewer and interviewee for just a few minutes at the end of the interview, you are allowing the person to talk about themself and they will likely feel flattered that you are interested. Plus, you can learn a lot about the company that you are hoping to intern with through their insight.

Before the interview ends, you should ask the interviewer when they will be making a decision on their internship hires. If your college has given you a deadline for securing an internship, then this is the time to bring up that date. If you feel uncomfortable in pushing, again point out the deadline and let them know (if this is true) that this is the internship you really want, but that you are talking to several other companies/studios just to make sure that you meet the college's deadline. Assuming the interviewer likes you, you've just put the suggestion that if they don't move quickly, they might lose you. A little healthy competition is a good thing.

Don't forget to thank the interviewer for their time and to thank the secretary or receptionist for their help as you leave.

## POINTS TO REMEMBER

- Keep good notes when you are in the process of searching for an interview. List dates and times of contact, who you spoke to and what they said. You'll need this for follow-up.
- Be polite to secretaries and receptionists. Enlist their help in getting messages or making contact with the person who handles internships.
- The "interview" starts the minute you walk into the building. Everything you say and do can contribute to whether or not you get the internship.
- Think of something interesting about yourself as a way to kick off the interview.
- Use questions during the interview to add additional information about yourself and your accomplishments.
- Ask questions about what you will be doing on the internship and ask for explanations on things that you do not understand.

# Chapter 5

# So We Talked . . .
# What Next?

- What to Do After the Internship
- Being Persistent Without being a Pest

You survived the interview and hopefully feel pretty good about it. If you were very fortunate, then you've already landed the internship. But with companies seeing so many applicants these days and the many laws and rules that have to be considered, companies tend to take their time before making offers to prospective interns.

So what's the next step? Say thank-you! The person you interviewed with gave you their time and they need to be thanked for doing it. Sure, you did say thank-you as you left the interview. That's expected. But a great way to stand out in the crowd is to again thank the person and this time, do it in more depth. The larger the group of applicants, the more important it is to stand out. This is also a great way to add any information about yourself, your goals or the skills that you forgot to talk about during the interview and remembered halfway home afterwards.

How important is it to thank the person you interviewed with for taking time out to talk to you? Critical! Many of the people that do the hiring of both interns and paid employees say that people who don't send a thank-you have seriously diminished their chances of getting the position. And according to an article in U.S. News and World Report only about 60 percent of the interviewees follow-up the interview with a thank-you of some kind.

There are a variety of ways to do it. You can send an email. It might read something like:

> "Thank-you so much for seeing me (earlier today/yesterday.) It was great to talk to a professional in the industry about my goals and to get a chance to see the (studio/station/facility.) I'm very excited about the possibility of interning with (name of company) and am very interested in (point out something or some area that was mentioned in the interview that you might be able to do or work on.) (If you forgot to tell them something about yourself you can put that here) I also meant to tell you that . . . I look forward to hearing from you soon. My cellphone is (number). Thanks again!"

The beauty of an email is that you can send it from the parking lot before you even start to drive away from the potential internship site. Seeing a thank-you show up in the person's inbox within an hour of your interview will go a long way in showing that you are the right person for the position.

If you met with more than one person, and it is likely that you did, they each deserve a thank-you. Make sure to customize your message by pointing out something specific that was said in the respective conversation. Cutting and pasting a generic email will be pretty obvious.

To make sure that you are ready to fire off those thank-you emails, make sure to get a card from each person so that you have the proper email address and spelling of their name.

While we are at it, there is one other person who may deserve a thank-you email from you. That would be the receptionist or secretary that you met when you first came into the office of the building. If you had a chance to talk with them a bit, a quick email saying it was nice to meet them, that you think the interview went well and you look forward to seeing them again soon can prove to be a very good move. After all, you will probably be talking to them again when you call and check to see if you got the internship. Keeping that relationship going can make getting back to the person in charge just that much easier.

You can also go splashier by sending the person you interviewed with something tangible. Flowers, a cookie basket, or something else along those lines. You certainly will be standing out and while it might sound like you're going overboard, if it helps to get the internship, you may consider it money well spent.

You need to decide if it's a good idea based on the personality of the person you are dealing with. If they are "all business", then you probably want to stick with the email. But if the person is someone that you really felt a connection with and who you enjoyed talking with, going this extra mile might make good sense.

No matter what you do, do it quickly. Again, email as soon as you leave the building and if you are going to send something, do it later that day and no later than the next day. After that basically says it was really an after-thought and gives the impression that you are not being sincere. Think about the last time you got a belated birthday wish. Did you think right off "Wow, this person actually forgot my birthday" rather than "I'm so glad this person remembered my birthday." Exactly! It made you think that you must not be so important to the person.

Same thing goes for the person who interviewed you. Too late and it really is better not to do it at all.

Here is where many prospective interns make a critical mistake. They wait for a call telling them they've got the internship. And they wait . . . and they wait.

This is not the time to wait! You know that your resumé was enough to get you into the running for the internship. You have already spent the time and effort on the interview. You need be proactive and continue to pursue the position.

Just because you have not heard back from the person does not mean that they are not interested in you for their internship position. They may be swamped at work, on vacation, or out sick. Don't make the dangerous assumption that you simply did not get the internship.

Get your notes out again, because you need to log your email and phone calls and attempts to reach the person you interviewed with, to keep track of what happens and what you say.

If you don't hear back from them within two days, drop them a quick email. They are likely seeing multiple people who want to intern with the company, not to mention doing the other parts of their job at the same time. You want to make sure you stay in that person's mind.

Your email doesn't have to be much more than:

> "I really enjoyed interviewing with you on (day of the week you interviewed with them.) Just wanted to drop you a note to let you know that I am still very interested in interning for (company/studio/station name.) My cellphone is (number.) Thanks, (your name)."

Take note that each email includes your cellphone number. A phrase that I often use is "Make it easy for me to contact you," meaning, don't make me look for your phone number or contact information. The easier you make it for someone to do what you want them to do, in this case hire you for the internship, the more likely they are to do it.

If at the end of the interview, the person gave you an idea of when they would be making their decision on who to bring on for their internship position, then several days before that date is when you would want to make your next contact.

If they didn't give you any specific date for their decision, wait another two days. If you still haven't heard back, it's time to make contact again. This time around, you can send another email or you can call the person.

The key with this contact is to let them know that there is an urgency to you getting an answer as to whether or not you have got the internship. Your college has likely given you a deadline to have your internship secured in order to get credit for the semester. Now is the time to remind the person who is hiring for the internship about that deadline.

You don't need to be concerned about telling the person that there is a deadline. The entertainment industry works on deadlines so this is not going to be anything new to the person you are contacting. Many people prioritize their work by deadlines, so by letting the other person know you are dealing with one may push them into a decision or letting you know if one has already been made.

If after another two days you have not received an answer, then it is time to make your final attempt. Again, this can be by email or by phone. You will want to again point out your deadline, but this time you will add another dimension. Let the person know that you are pursuing several other internships, but the one with their company is your number one choice. So you would appreciate it if they would let you know if you are still in the running or if you aren't, so that you can pursue one of your other options.

What you have done this time is to let the person know that this internship is very important to you. Not just because you need to do one or because you need the credits to graduate, but that it is the internship that you really want. You have also let them know that you are in demand by telling them that you are being looked at for other internships. You've put the notion in their mind that if they do not offer you the position rather quickly, you may accept one with another company and they would lose you. Any thing or person that is in demand is automatically a more sought after commodity.

If you still do not hear back after this, then at this point it is relatively safe to believe that you didn't get the internship and the person simply is not showing you the courtesy of letting you know.

Remember, at no point during these post-interview exchanges should you get pushy or testy with the individual. You need to remain positive and courteous even if you are not getting the response that you want . . . or any response at all. You will find that the entertainment business is a rather small universe and you do not want to have to explain years later why you sent a very rude email or were discourteous during a phone call. It is not out of the question that somewhere down the road you will encounter this person again.

If the internship that you did not get is one that you might want to do later or the company is one that you hope to work for someday, there is no harm in attempting to keep in contact with the person you interviewed with at that company. Once you have landed an internship elsewhere, consider sending a quick email to that person letting them know where you will be interning.

If you are still interested in interning with that company, let them know. The person who got that internship may not work out and you will get a call. There can be a real advantage to doing more than one internship as you prepare to transition into the workforce. We'll discuss that in a later chapter.

The competition for internships can be high and you cannot let yourself get depressed if you do not land one that you really wanted. Since you probably do need one to get your degree or certificate, it is important to apply to more than one so that you increase your odds of being able to meet this requirement.

In most cases, nearly every quality internship will give you new insights and opportunities to help ready yourself for an entry level position in the entertainment industry.

The key to getting an internship, as well as getting any job that you will go for during your career, is to be persistent. Remember that just because someone has not got back to you, does not mean that they are not interested in you. They simply may have got busy. Keep making contact and letting them know that you are still interested and available. You may be surprised what could happen weeks or even months down the road.

## POINTS TO REMEMBER

- Thank the person you interviewed with, both at the end of the interview in person and within 24 hours following the interview by email or possibly with a gift.
- Always include your contact information in every communication with the interviewer.
- Follow-up quickly and often.
- Keep notes about your follow-up.
- Use deadlines, but always be polite about them.

# Part 3

# During the Internship

# Chapter 6

# I'm Here . . . Now What?

- Preparing for the Big Day
- What to Do on the First Day of Your Internship

The first day of your internship is obviously going to be a nervous one. But it's also going to be an exciting day. It's actually the first day of your career.

One key to making it awesome is planning. To make sure that everything goes right that day, it's important to do a few things ahead of time.

Decide what you are going to wear. You made a good impression on the person who interviewed you, but now you are going to be meeting many of the other people on the staff where you are doing your internship. Just as the first impression was important at your interview, it's important again with everyone else at the station, so the same clothing and appearance guidelines as we discussed in Chapter 2 apply.

Being on time is always going to be crucial and you absolutely don't want to be late on your first day. If you want to be taken seriously at your internship, you need to show that you take *it* seriously. One of the best ways is to be on time. You want to get off on the right foot.

Take a note pad and pen with you and use them. You will probably be getting a lot of new information all at once on your first day. Everything from door entrance codes to instructions on how to do various tasks. Write this information down. One of the keys to success at your internship is to be autonomous. That means that you handle things on your own. It's hard to do if you have to ask for simple information over and over again.

Ask questions. There's a saying that goes 'There's no such thing as a dumb question." Well, that may not be totally true. There are some really dumb questions out there. But asking questions is also an important part of learning. If you don't understand something that you are being told or shown, there is no shame in admitting it. You're an intern and learning is what you are there to do. If you already knew everything and were good at it, you wouldn't be interning, you'd already be working at your first job.

It is far better to ask questions in order to get a clear understanding of something that you will be expected to do than to not ask and either do it wrong or not be able to do it at all. And you'll find that most people actually like it when you ask questions. It shows that you are interested and are paying attention.

You're going to be meeting a lot of people and it's important to remember their names and their positions. Again, writing them down is the key. You don't want to do it while you are being introduced to them, but do it as soon as possible so you don't forget. It is really impressive to people that you have just met when you can refer to them by name the next time you come into contact with them. Remembering and using a person's name shows respect and makes a positive and lasting impression, which is exactly what you are trying to do at your new internship.

There are a couple of things that you do not want to do on your first day or on any day at your internship for that matter. These include talking on or using your cellphone. You are there to learn and being seen texting or heard making personal calls does not show that you are there for the right reason. Save that sort of thing for your lunch break or after you are done for the day and have left your internship.

Internships in the entertainment field are different from those in other industries in quite a few ways. One of the most important concerns the people involved. Depending on the area or department you work in, you may have access to well-known people or celebrities. And while it may be exciting to see or meet them, you need to act appropriately. Keep in mind that they are at work, just as you are, and not at a personal appearance. If you are introduced to them, it's fine to mention how much you admire their work but asking for an autograph or to take a picture with them is absolutely something you want to avoid doing. When you're at your internship, you want to be looked at as a professional in the industry and not a fan.

The person who interviewed and hired you for your internship is probably not going to be your internship supervisor. More often than not, you will be working with someone else who you will meet for the first time on that first day. This is another great time to ask questions.

Some of the things that you want to make sure and find out include:

- What days and times you will be working.
- If you are going to be there for more than four hours in a day, when should you take your lunch break.
- What specifically will be some of your tasks and responsibilities.
- Where you can put your personal items.

- What number should you call in the rare case that you can't make it to your internship.
- Your supervisor's contact information.

If there are any problems with anything, such as the days or times that you are scheduled to work, you want to resolve those right away. As much as we use social media these days, this is not the place to put information intended for your internship supervisor. Calling in sick or letting them know that you are going to be late should be done by phone and if you do not reach the person directly, leave a voice mail and follow it up with an email. It is your responsibility to make sure that your message is received, so you might also want to let the receptionist at your internship know or make a follow up call a short time later.

The first day on your internship will likely consist of mostly watching and listening and of course, writing things down. As with any new situation, it takes time to feel comfortable and feel like you belong. Don't worry if you don't accomplish much on that first day.

## POINTS TO REMEMBER

- It's ok to be nervous. Everyone is on their first day.
- Dress to impress. You will be meeting a lot of new people.
- Be on time.
- Behave professionally. While the work product may be fun, this is still a business.
- Ask questions and write down information.
- Work to remember the names and positions of the people you meet.
- Get the contact information for your supervisor.
- Never use social media to communicate important information to your supervisor such as having to miss a day.

# Chapter 7

# Getting Noticed Without Making a Scene

- I've Made it . . . or Have I?
- How to Become Part of the Team
- Keep Private Things Private

An internship is a step, a first step in your career in the entertainment industry. It is not an elevator. You don't get on and simply go straight to the top. Like steps, you need to climb each one.

Perhaps one of the most dangerous things that can happen during in internship is that the person starts to think that just because they are working at a station, or studio, or other facility in the business, they have made it. The truth of the matter is far from it. Sitting back and waiting for that ride to the top to happen is the best way to get stuck exactly where you are.

It is easy to get caught up in what is going on around you. But you need to keep a level head and remain realistic about what you are doing. While some internships result in jobs, more do not. Stay focused, continue with your college classes if you are an undergraduate and remember that you still have a lot to learn.

Nearly everything in the entertainment industry works on a deadline. Sometimes, as in the case of a TV or film shoot, it may seem like just the opposite, with seemingly endless takes and retakes. But whether it is obvious or not, there are deadlines being observed and met.

With people working sometimes at furious paces, it's easy to feel like you are being overlooked as an intern. So how do you become part of the team and get noticed?

The key is to *make* yourself a part of the team. Your internship is likely only a semester long so you really don't have time to wait to be invited. Show you fit in.

Treat your internship like you would any other paying job. After all, you want to show the company that you are ready to work. With the exception of other interns, everyone you come into contact with will be a professional, so follow the same rules they're expected to follow. This includes your work habits, dress, behavior, and attitude.

Some people think that as long as they get their job done and do everything else correctly, being late now and again is alright. Not so! It's interesting how being late for work and appointments can actually overshadow how good you are at your job. While there are going to be those rare times that you can't avoid being late, such as when you get stuck in traffic or have car trouble, they need to be few and far between.

Reliability is a major part of being successful in any industry and the entertainment industry is not any different. In fact, in some ways, being where you are supposed to be when you are supposed to be there is even more important in this field. Because of the nature of the business, it is very hard to cover for someone whose absence is not expected.

Just like arriving on time is important, leaving on time is equally not important. Be willing to stay past your scheduled ending time if there is something big in the works. When employees stay overtime to work on a project, it's usually a sure bet that they are running into problems or running tight on deadlines. Even if you don't feel like you may have much to to contribute getting the job done, the fact that you offered to stay and help will score major points with the paid employees and your supervisor as well. It really is an awful feeling to be up against the clock on something and gradually watch your fellow employees leave. The ones who stay, especially when they don't have to, really make an impression.

Be personable. I tell my interns to make sure that people know they are there. This doesn't mean to make yourself known by being boisterous or showing off. But you want to make sure that you don't end up sitting in a corner by yourself either.

Talk to people. Don't be timid. Ask people questions or just make conversation if the time is right. You don't want to take up too much of their time; after all they are on the job and have deadlines to meet. Pick the right times to talk like in the break room or ask to walk with someone when they are going from one point to another.

Elevators are a great place to chit-chat. One intern recently related an experience he had while riding the elevator at his internship. He found himself alone with a woman he had never met before. Rather than ride in silence, he introduced himself as the company's new intern. She told him her name and they started talking. He told her about his school and the fact that he was about to graduate and she asked him things like what area of the business he wanted to pursue. They had a nice exchange. Later he mentioned to someone that he had met a really nice woman in the elevator. It turns out she was the general manager! Because he was not shy, he accomplished a fantastic introduction with one of the most important people in the company.

Not all the jobs assigned to an intern are exciting or even, for that matter, important. Interns are often asked to do menial tasks such as going out for coffee or filing things. We all know that's not exactly what you went there to do, but as long as you are also doing things that are of value to your ultimate goal, then you can just chalk up these lesser tasks as part of "paying your dues."

Rapper Snoop Dogg once said, "If it's flipping hamburgers at McDonald's, be the best hamburger flipper in the world. Whatever it is you do, you have to master your craft."

He couldn't be more right. We all did menial tasks at one time or another during the beginning stages of our careers. It's just part of the process. And while it might sound silly at first, if you think about it, delivering coffee to people is a great way to get to meet them. There really can be an opportunity in even the most mundane aspect of your internship if you just make an effort to find it.

Sometimes the jobs interns are asked to handle are just down right funny. Several years ago a student of mine was able to get an internship on one of the most popular sitcoms on TV at the time. Her career goal was to be a director or producer. Instead she found herself doing a variety of rather interesting errands for the Show Runner. Among them was taking care of one of the star's dogs on the days he brought him to the set, taking a ping pong table to the home of one of the other stars and setting it up so she could learn how to play ping pong for an upcoming scene, and, my personal favorite, returning clothing items for a woman who had a recurrent role on the series. The woman liked to shop but apparently didn't like to try things on, so she would just buy whatever she saw that she liked and then hand off what didn't work out to interns to return for her.

That last one does stretch the role of an intern nearly to the breaking point, but it's just an example of the kind of bizarre things that you might encounter on your internship. By the way, that young intern has gone on to a very successful career in television as a writer and producer.

Volunteering for jobs that aren't all that popular is a good way to establish your value as a team player. It's not uncommon

that interns who do some of the more routine tasks find themselves offered some of the more prized assignments as a sort of
reward.

No matter how small the job is, you need to do it willingly
and do it well. You may be surprised at how this simple approach
can help to unlock the door to you doing more of the things
you want to do at your internship. No one wants to be around
someone who is grouchy and doing their work begrudgingly.
It's an impression that once made, is hard to get rid of. Start
things off right and remember, you won't be doing these menial
tasks forever.

A big part of fitting in is to know what is going on around
you. It's likely you are not at your internship 40 hours a week,
so things can change between your assigned days. It's the same
for people who work part-time in the business. If possible, see
if you can get an email address with the company. You should
have one anyway as a way of keeping in touch with your
internship coordinator, but it's a great way to keep up-to-date
with things going on at the company. Even if you don't use it
much for communicating, just checking it out over the days
that you are not working will give you access to information
like big events, personnel changes, and a wide variety of other
topics.

If the company has a Facebook page or uses Twitter, friend
and follow those as well. Anything that will keep you up-to-
date with what's going on at the company on the days that you
are not there will help you to fit in with the overall flow of the
organization.

You are going to be privy to quite a bit of information at
your internship, the "inside" info if you will. As tempting as
this kind of info may be to share with friends and on social
media, it is absolutely something that you do not to do.

You may be asked to sign a Trade Secret Disclosure form or
something similar at your internship. Basically it is a legal promise

that you will not share information about the company that it does not want made public. This is something that needs to be taken very seriously. Hollywood works on the concept of "smoke and mirrors" and none of us are supposed to share the secrets of how things are done.

Another area that should be kept confidential is personal information that we may learn about other people in the business . . . especially celebrities or other well-known individuals. Trust is a big deal and you don't want to get the reputation of being someone that people can't be comfortable speaking around for fear of you disseminating that information either in conversation or on social media.

It's also important to keep up with the product your internship produces. If you're interning at a radio station, listen to the programming. At a TV station, watch the shows and newscasts. You get the idea. What is happening on the air or on the screen is likely to be a topic around "the office" and you want to be able to get in on the conversation if you have the chance. It's a great way to not only help you feel like you fit in, but it also shows your supervisors and others at your internship site that you are keeping up with what matters.

The same goes for the industry in general. Your internship makes you a part of the business and you want to know what is going on with it. There are a great many websites that you can check on a regular basis that will help keep you in the know. That way if something big is going on in the industry and someone asks you what you think about it, hopefully you will know what they are talking about, be able to show your knowledge and engage in a meaningful conversation about the matter.

Once you get comfortable at your internship and have developed some working relationships, it might be time to start sharing some of your ideas. You probably have a lot of them.

Make sure that they are well thought out before you present them.

When formulating any idea, one important step is to look for possible ramifications or legal implications. These all need to be thought out and resolved beforehand. Create different scenarios around your idea that will help you determine a variety of possible outcomes. You don't want to present an idea only to have the other person point out very quickly the obvious reason that it won't work or couldn't/shouldn't be done. While you obviously can't think of everything, you can make a concerted effort to be thorough before you present your idea.

Be ready for your idea to be rejected. It happens to the best of us, and more often than most of us would probably like to admit. Your idea may not be a bad one, it might just not be the right time to try it. If your idea is rejected, ask why and solicit ideas that might make it better and more viable.

Remember, it was your idea that was rejected, not you. Do not take it personally and don't let it stop you from coming up with new ideas and presenting them. Who knows, your next one just might be the one that makes it.

## POINTS TO REMEMBER

- Make yourself a part of the team by acting like you belong.
- Treat your internship like a paying job. Be on time and act professionally.
- Treat every task assigned to you as important, even if it isn't.
- Keep up with what is happening at the company you are working with and the industry in general.
- Keep from sharing information that is not supposed to be public.

# Chapter 8

# Pro-Active Interning—
# Making the Most of Your
# Internship

- Making the Most of Your Internship
- Ethical Interning

Your internship is going to be basically as good as you make it. You have a limited time at your internship site so you want to do as much as you possibly can while making a lasting impression on the people who may be able to help you in the future.

One of the most common reasons that companies give for not offering internships is that interns need too much supervision and they simply don't have the time to keep an eye on them or find things to keep them busy. That's why you want to be pro-active on your internship.

You basically have two missions during your internship. You want to show the company and your supervisors what you have to offer. At the same time, you want to learn more about your craft. Whether either one or both happens is at least partially up to you.

Find out who the major players are at your internship. Check out the station's website to find out who the important people are and what they look like. If their pictures are not shown, search Facebook or the Internet using their name and company to see them and to learn about their jobs.

No matter how shy or out of place you might feel, you need to make sure you are noticed. Not by being loud or boastful. Those are absolutely not the ways to do it. One intern found his tenure ending very quickly when he basically told everyone he worked with at his internship that he could show them better ways to do most everything. Even if he actually had been right, the attitude that he was there to save the day did not go over well with people who had been successfully working in the industry for years and his internship came to an abrupt end.

Keep in mind that everyone you encounter knows a lot more about the business than you do at this point, so don't try to get into a one-up-manship match. You will lose and look bad in doing it.

When you are at your internship, talk to people. Say hello, introduce yourself and tell them that you are the new intern. If the person is involved in an area that you know you want to explore more closely while you are involved at the work site, let them know that as well. You don't have to go into much detail. Say something like "I am really interested in production and have good ProTools skills. I would really like to sit in and watch what you do at some point if that would be ok." You are setting this up as an opportunity down the road.

You will find that people are generally flattered when someone asks to watch what they do and acknowledges that they are the expert in their area.

Be willing to learn everything, even if you think you will never use the skill or the area is one that is really not on your radar as a career. Go out of your comfort zone and challenge yourself in areas that you have not explored before. It all goes with trying to get the most out of your internship. The more skills you gain and the more areas that you are skilled in will make you that much more employable when the time comes.

Keep in mind that while taking the initiative to talk to people in areas you want to explore further and then sitting in with them to watch and learn is great, it does not mean that you can ignore the assignments that have been given to you by your internship supervisor. Your first responsibility is to do whatever tasks are assigned to you and to do them well. When you are done, look around and see what else might need doing. If it is something that you know how to do already, let whoever you are working with know that you are happy to jump in and get it done. If you don't already know how to do it, ask for someone to show you. Of all the things that have impressed me during my career in working with interns, this one is right at the top. It is such a great skill to be able to recognize something that needs to be done without anyone having to tell you and such a great help to have someone offer to take care of it!

Once you have been shown how to do a task, tell your supervisor that you are happy to take care of that job each time that you come in if it needs to be done. That's pro-active interning. It's hard to find a person who is not impressed by someone who wants to do more at work. And now you have a task that you can lay claim to. Do it well each time you come in and you are really part of the team.

Feedback is important and you want to seek it out whenever you can whether it is good or bad. If someone tells you that you did a good job on something, thank them and ask them specifically what they liked about your work. The same thing should go for situations where your work is not given praise. Find out exactly what was wrong or wasn't done well. This way you can continue doing the things that you are doing well and change or eliminate the things that you have not been doing at your best level. It's far more valuable than just being praised for your efforts or not. A great saying that I once heard from a very successful person was "Find out what you do well and then do a whole lot of it." Makes good sense, doesn't it!

Your internship is also a time to continue building your demo or portfolio. Ask for produced versions of commercials you have written or perhaps voiced, get copies of audio or video that you had a hand in producing, keep documentation of projects that you were a part of.

And don't forget to take pictures. A word of caution here. You don't want to be known as the intern with the camera. Many people do not like to have their pictures taken when they are not aware of it or have not given their permission to be photographed. But pictures from your internship are great to use on websites and social media.

Before you start though, talk with your on-site supervisor and get their approval. You will want to have a clear understanding of the areas where it is ok to shoot and areas that you should avoid.

For example, if you are interning on the set of a movie, it will probably not be ok to take pictures while the cameras are rolling. Many directors don't want anything leaking out until they are ready for what they are filming to be public. And you would want to refrain from taking pictures of yourself on the set or with any of the props. But you could still get some great shots. Things like a picture of yourself outside the studio gates, what you are having for lunch at the commissary, exteriors on the studio lot . . . all of which will look great to document your internship.

Timing is important on all of this. Give yourself three or four weeks to settle into the internship and for people working at the site get to know you. Once you feel comfortable and are able to walk in and say "hi" to people and they say "hi" to you, take that as a signal to start taking more initiative in becoming involved in new areas and with new people.

There are limits as to what an intern can do, so not all jobs will likely be open to you. There are several reasons for this. First are the conditions set forth in the Fair Labor Standards Act from Chapter One. Then there are the unions. The entertainment industry is rife with unions and one of their biggest interests is in preserving jobs for their members. There really is literally a union for just about any job that you can think of.

When a job or task is covered by a union, only a union member can do that job. There's no wriggle room on this. Allowing a non-union person to do the work can result in the company being hit with a very large fine. And it's hard to figure out sometimes what is a union task and what isn't. While it might seem nit-picky, union rules can be very strict about who does something as simple as move something on the stage of a TV show or adjust a person's microphone. There is no rule though on an intern sitting in to watch. You can learn a lot from just watching and talking to the person who is doing the job.

If this is something that you want to do, then check with your supervisor for permission. It's also a good idea to ask the person you would be sitting in with as well. Most of the time you will find that, if approached correctly, the majority of the people at your internship site will be very happy to interact with you and often will take you under their wing if you show that you are enthusiastic and professional.

Don't be afraid to ask for what you want. You don't want to rely on someone to figure out what experiences you should have and offer them to you. If you go to your supervisor with some ideas, chances are they will likely be fine with them and will probably be impressed with your initiative. You also have a great opportunity to let them know that you understand the business. Do your homework and find out what jobs are covered by unions and which ones are not. If you are talking about an area where a union is involved, you may be able to score some points by letting them know that you are aware of the limitations, but you are still interested in observing just the same.

So where can you actually get your hands on some real work? This is something you need to work with your intern supervisor on. Set up an appointment to go in and talk to them about your progress. About the fifth or sixth week is usually an excellent time to do this. By this time, you should have already established yourself as a reliable and competent intern.

At the appointment, let your supervisor know that you are enjoying your internship and again thank them for giving you the opportunity. Go over your skills with them. Although you did this initially when you were interviewing for the internship, your supervisor probably doesn't remember them all. And let them know that you are interested in putting more of those skills to work. It's a good idea to go in with a plan so that if you are asked what you want to do, you have some answers in mind.

Having the plan in writing allows you to give it to your supervisor for them to consider later. They probably will want to give your ideas some thought and they also may want to keep it for further reference as you continue with your internship.

Be realistic when you make your plan. If you are interning at a radio station, you are not going to get your own show. At a TV station, you won't be covering an evening on the anchor desk. And you won't find yourself behind the camera filming a scene in a movie. Keep the areas that you ask to work in within the entry-level areas; ones that are suitable to your expertise in the industry.

Here's what it might look like:

## Idea Plan

**The idea:** (Briefly describe your idea.) "I would like to do a series on the job prospects for college students who do internships versus students who don't do them."

**What makes this a good idea?** Colleges have been raising tuitions recently and students are trying to finish quicker but at the same time hoping that they are going to be able to find a job quickly once they graduate.

**Who is the audience?** College students, high school students, parents of students, employers.

**What do we need to do it?** Contact with college professors who supervise interns, several interns, and some employers who have had interns and hired graduates who did internships while still in school. Some economic data, if available, showing that graduates who do internships get hired faster and paid more than graduates who don't.

**How long will it take to get the project ready?** (This is just an estimate . . . but be sure to give yourself enough time to *really* get the work done.)

**What would your role in the project be?** (Would you coordinate the project? Do the interviews or writing? Do the editing or production? It doesn't matter what you see your role as, but you need to be clear as to what you see yourself doing in connection with the project.)

## POINTS TO REMEMBER

- You need to make sure that you are getting out of your internship what you want.
- Do your homework and find out what key people at your internship site do and what they look like.
- Look for opportunities to help out even if that work has not been assigned to you. But ask permission before doing anything.
- Schedule a time to meet with your internship coordinator to go over your goals and ask for more opportunities.
- Understand that due to union rules and labor laws, not everything at your internship site will be available to you to explore.
- Be realistic in your expectations of what areas you will be able to work in.

# Chapter 9

# What Can Go Wrong Usually Does—What To Do About it

- So You Made Your First Mistake
- Dealing with Difficult People—Where Do You Stand?
- Where to Draw the Line

Mistakes happen no matter how carefully you do things, whether you are working on a job or at an internship. Nobody is perfect. So what do you do when the inevitable happens?

If you make a mistake, it's always a good idea to own up to it. Denying a mistake that later is linked to you puts you in the very difficult situation of not only having to deal with the mistake, but the fallout from trying to distance yourself from it.

When you are talking about the error with your supervisor, keep from making excuses. There really is not an acceptable reason for making a mistake. Bottom line is, you messed up. Excuses won't make that go away. What is acceptable is to explain how the error happened and what you are going to do to make sure that something like it never happens again. If you can learn by a mistake, then at least something positive has come from the error.

Will you lose your internship over it? Probably not. Unless it was intentional or fueled by something that you should not have been doing on the internship such as drinking. If you handle it correctly it should not result in anything more than a discussion with your supervisor. That person knows that you are new and still learning. This is also one of the reasons that you should not expect to be handed high-level work to do at your internship. You just aren't ready yet . . . your time will come.

Obviously, no one wants to make a mistake and as an intern, you probably won't be in a position to make a major one. But it could happen if you take charge when you don't have the authority to do so. Take this case from 2013. A summer intern at the National Transportation Safety Administration, or NTSB, who was supposed to simply be answering the phones and passing media inquiries along to the appropriate people, went outside the scope of his authority. The intern erroneously confirmed for KTVU TV in San Francisco, California, the names of several of the pilots on Asiana Flight 214, which had crashed at San Francisco International Airport and killed two girls from China. The station went on the air with the names, which turned out to be not only fake, but very racist.

That intern was fired and KTVU TV apologized on the air, noting that they had confirmed the names with the NTSB. To date, no one has ever confirmed where the names actually originated.

But even a small mistake can make you feel very embarrassed. There are two pro-active ways to protect yourself from making an error as best you can.

First, if you don't know how to do something or are unsure about how to do it right, ASK! You've heard the phrase "there is no such thing as a dumb question". Well it's not quite true. The dumb question is the one you didn't ask that you should have. You don't necessarily have to admit you don't know how to do something. Instead, you can just say you are checking to make sure you are doing it right. Basically it's the same thing, but the latter keeps you from looking and feeling like you don't know what you are doing.

Secondly, check, check, and double-check your work. It's a habit you will want to practice throughout your entire career. One extra check might just be what's needed to catch a mistake before it goes too far to correct it in time.

People in the entertainment industry are an interesting group of people. And they are often working under an extreme amount of pressure. This can cause them to be short and perhaps a little rude at times. Learning to deal with this variety of personalities is one of the most important parts of your internship and one of the reasons that employers want you to have done at least one or even two internships before you get that entry-level job.

Most of the time when tempers flare, people are responding more to the situation and not so much to the person involved. It's not uncommon to hear some harsh words and then ten minutes later find the people involved are working together as if nothing happened.

Of course, that is not always the case. There are difficult people working in every industry. These are the people that you want to avoid. Aligning yourself with someone who is difficult or negative and that other employees try not to be around will cast you in a negative light. Sadly these are often the people who will be most welcoming to an intern as they don't really have an active social base of other people at their jobs. While they might need your company, it is better for you not to spend much more time than necessary with them.

Sometimes you have no choice. The person could be your boss at the internship or they could be the person you are assigned to work with. As an intern, you may not know where you stand when you find yourself working with or for a difficult or mean person. The bottom line is that everyone deserves respect no matter where you are in the hierarchy of a company. If you feel you are not being treated fairly and that feeling persists, you do need to take steps to resolve it.

If what is going on does not stop on its own, then the best first step is to try and talk to the other person and see if you can find out what's at the root of the problem. Do this in private and not during a flurry of activity on the job. Try to set up a time to talk to them during a break or at lunch. Ask them if you are doing something wrong or doing something that is bothering them. You may find that they have no idea what you are talking about and that they weren't even aware they were sending negative signals your way.

On the other hand, there might actually be a problem and you have now opened an opportunity to talk about it and learn from it. Be open to what the other person has to say. Let them know that you understand and will work on doing a better job. Often this leads to a much better working situation since they now know that you care about what you are doing as an intern.

Any time that you have an issue with someone at your internship, it's important to keep notes detailing what happened and what was said. This way you don't have to rely on your memory if you have to take the matter to someone else to resolve. You should also make the internship coordinator at your school aware of the situation. At some point, they may want to or need to get involved. Ultimately, they are responsible for you at your internship, so it's important to keep them in the loop, even if you don't need their help yet.

You need to talk to the supervisor at your internship about the issue. Let them know what is going on and tell them that you have tried to resolve the problem yourself. Detail what you have done and when you did it.

At this point, leave it up to that person to handle the situation. Go about your internship as you normally would and continue to treat the other person involved with the respect and professionalism you do everyone else at your internship site.

If the problem continues, now is the likely time for the internship coordinator at your college to get involved. Just as you did with your on-site supervisor, let them know that you have tried to resolve the problem yourself as well, and have already got your supervisor at the site involved. Using your notes, give them complete details. They will need to know everything that has happened when they contact your internship and talk to your supervisor there.

In some cases, the resolution may be to have you move to a different department or begin working with someone else at your internship. If that happens, do not take it personally. Not everyone enjoys working with newcomers to the industry and some people are just harder to get along with than others.

The difficult part is that you are at the internship and your coordinator is not. That is why it is so important to bring them into the situation quickly if something that is either illegal or immoral is going on at your internship site. This could involve either employees or other interns.

Among the situations that would require immediate involvement of your internship coordinator:

- The use of alcohol or drugs at your internship.
- People offering you alcohol or drugs at your internship.
- Being pressured to go to parties or other places that you don't want to go.
- Unwanted physical attention.
- Improper comments or actions.

None of these things are acceptable and need to be dealt with quickly. You don't need to participate in things of this nature in order to keep your internship or to have a better chance at getting a job at the end of your internship.

## Points to Remember

- Mistakes happen to everyone.
- Own up to your mistake, don't make excuses for it.
- Learn from your mistakes.
- Try to deal with difficult people by talking to them about the problem and how to resolve it.
- Go to your internship supervisor if you need further help.
- Report unethical or illegal activities your internship coordinator immediately.

# Part 4

# After the Internship

# Chapter 10

# Keeping it All in Perspective

- How to Know When to Leave
- Turning the Internship into a Job
- The Internship is Only the Beginning

One of the hardest things to do for many interns is to leave!

You've got comfortable at the company and know what to do . . . and hopefully you've been enjoying the experience.

There is always the possibility that you may be able to stay on at the company, either as a part-time or full-time employee. If you think about it, you have already proven that you are a valuable person to the company. Plus, you have already gone through several months of training (without pay) and may be much more ready to work for the company in an entry-level position as opposed to someone from the outside who is newly hired.

You should start thinking about this before the end of your internship, while you still have access to the facility and the staff. Giving yourself at least four weeks allows you time to start talking to people and making appointments to meet.

If you would like to remain with the company, you need to let people know that. If there is someone who you have been working with closely and who you know is impressed with your work, ask them if they would feel comfortable recommending you for a position. That recommendation could go a long way in changing your internship into employment.

Make an appointment as well to talk to your internship supervisor. Remind them that your internship is close to coming to an end. They actually may have forgotten the date. Let them know that you are enjoying the experience and don't be afraid to tell them that you would like to stay with the company.

Ask for what you want! Too often we hint around at the point, hoping the other person will be able to figure out what we are getting at. It doesn't always work and then you can come up empty handed. So don't be afraid to come right out and say that you would like to work for the company and ask if there are any job openings that you would be qualified for.

Be ready to point out your accomplishments during the internship, the different departments you have worked in, areas in which you feel competent to work, and ways in which you have distinguished yourself from any other interns. You may also want to point out your attendance and punctuality during your internship.

You are selling yourself to the company, so don't be shy when it comes to talking about yourself and your accomplishments. Make sure your supervisor sees that you are an asset to the organization and that you are doing valuable work that will be missed.

Hopefully, a job will be open already or soon to open and you will have an inside track to getting it. If not, ask your supervisor to keep you in mind and to let you know when an opening does come up.

You may be asked to stay on as an intern for longer than your original scheduled internship. After all, you have been contributing and are part of the team. If you are still learning things at your internship, then you may want to stay. After all, that was the purpose of doing your internship. However, if you continue to do the things that you have mastered and you have gotten all you think you can from the experience, it is time to move on, either to another internship or to an entry-level job.

There is no reason not to be very frank about this with your supervisor. Let them know that you would very much like to stay on with the company, but since your internship will be complete you will no longer be receiving college credit and that you simply cannot continue to work for free. Most people will easily understand that you, just like everyone else, have bills to pay.

A word of caution. Because you have made yourself a valuable part of the company, they will likely not want to lose you. You're doing good work and you've been doing it without pay. Be careful that you are not lured into staying by the promise of a job down the road. While a job may come up, if you are qualified for it and the company would like to hire you for it, you should not have to continue your internship to be in line for the position.

If you are going to be leaving the company at the end of your internship, ask your supervisor and other employees that you have got to know if it is ok to use them as a reference, either at your next internship or when you start applying for jobs. Having people who are actually in the business as references will make your next application stand out.

If you can get them to write you a letter of recommendation, those are always nice to have when you start looking for a job, entry-level or otherwise. Some companies are no longer willing to write reference letters for legal reasons. But when you can get them, you should. Some companies prefer them to you providing a list of names and phone numbers that they then have to call. A letter from someone actually in the business describing your work ethic and declaring that you have what it takes to make it in the industry can be invaluable when you start looking for a paid position. If you can get your letters in advance, you can save yourself a lot of scrambling to get them when you are facing a deadline.

Your internship is going to fly by! But it really is only the beginning for you.

By the end of your internship you will have had the chance to:

- Figure out how all the various subjects you studied in school come together.
- See how the industry works in person.
- Hone some of your skills.
- Learn what skills you need to improve.
- Work with industry professionals.
- Create some valuable professional relationships for the future.

## POINTS TO REMEMBER

- Make an appointment with your internship supervisor about four weeks before your internship ends to talk about the possibility of staying on as a paid employee.
- If the contracted time at your internship is over and you are no longer learning anything, then it is time to leave.
- Be careful not to let a promise of a job keep you at an internship if you are not continuing to learn.
- Ask for permission to list people at your internship as references and get letters if you can.
- Assess your skills and work readiness at the end of your internship.

# Chapter 11

# You Got In—Don't Let Yourself Fall Out

- What Happens Next?
- Keeping Your Contacts Alive

Based on your assessment of your internship, you will have a much better indicator of whether or not you are ready to enter the job force. You need to ask yourself whether you feel competent to take on the duties of the people you have studied and worked with. Be realistic with yourself. You want your first paid job to be a success.

This is not a race. You may decide that you need additional training and want to take more college classes or do more work at your college radio or TV station or in their production studios. That's fine.

Immediately after completing your internship, send a thank-you to your supervisor and anyone who was important to your success in completing it. You can do this by email, but even in this age of everything electronic, it means much more to a person to receive a handwritten card or note. It certainly will stand out and not get buried under the daily barrage of emails. It doesn't have to be anything elaborate. Simply thank them for their time and the opportunity to learn from them during your internship. It's not only common courtesy but will also serve to keep them from forgetting you.

Update your resumé. You now have actual industry experience to put on it. Put your internship right at the top of your experience section and list some of the departments or projects that you worked on.

It's a good practice to update your resumé every time you have something to add to it. At some point, you will also start dropping off older or less important items. The key is to have an up-to-date resumé ready to go at all times. That way you will not have to scramble to update it when you need it and risk missing the chance to add something important.

You also may decide to do another internship. Perhaps it will be in a different area of entertainment this time. Internships are a great way to get a look at a different aspect of the industry as you try and figure out just where you fit in best and where you will be most successful. Employers often favor prospective employees who have done more than one internship because they have gone an additional step in preparing themselves. And of course, it's another great way to add to your list of contacts.

Contacts are very important in the entertainment field. They are truly worth their weight in gold. You made some at your first internship and you want to make sure that you keep them. It's really not hard.

If there was a potential job brewing before you left your internship, you will certainly want to call your internship supervisor to check on it. You don't want to wait for them to call you. In this fast moving business, people get forgotten. So with a job on the line, make sure you stay "top of mind" with whoever does the hiring.

Otherwise, you can stay in touch by simply keeping people up-to-date with what is going on. A quick email will do the trick. You can use holidays or other occasions to drop them a line, let them know what grade you got in your internship class, or ask their advice on what classes they think you should take if you are continuing in your college program. You will find that asking people for their opinions also lets them know that you value their expertise and can be a great way of ingratiating yourself to them.

All of these things will keep them from forgetting you and make it much easier to ask them for a reference down the road. It's hard to ask a person for a favor, and you are much less likely to get it, if that person hasn't heard from you in a long time.

## POINTS TO REMEMBER

- Assess your entry-level job readiness at the conclusion of your internship.
- Consider doing a second internship at another company or perhaps in another area of the entertainment industry.
- Immediately after your internship, send a thank-you to your supervisor and other people who helped make your internship a success.
- Update your resumé to show your internship experience.
- Keep your contacts alive by staying in touch with them.

# Conclusion

What you initially thought of as only a requirement for graduation or working for free, you are now hopefully looking at as an amazing opportunity. Your internship can be the "key to the kingdom" if you just choose to look at it that way.

Thinking of your internship as a long audition for a job will give you the prospective needed to make the most of the experience and end up with good references or perhaps even a position.

Your internship is a time to evaluate your skills and also explore more of the entertainment industry. While you may have gone into the internship with a pretty solid idea of what you wanted as a career, it never hurts to keep your options open and try something new. You may discover that it is a better fit for you. You might also be glad that you had at least an introduction to the job and its required skills years down the road when a new opportunity presents itself.

As with most industries, the more you know the better off you are. The entertainment industry is no different. Having skills in a multiple of areas makes you not only more employable but also more apt to keep your job and advance. So take the time now, while you have it, to expand your capabilities.

We look at internships as a college-level experience for the most part, aimed at helping a person get that first, entry-level job. But an internship is something that can be done at any time during your career. You will find people well along in their professions, doing an internship as a way of gaining new skills and exploring different parts of the industry. They know the advantage of learning hands-on in the actual workplace environment and the benefit of meeting people in an on-the-job setting.

Whether you are just starting out in the field of entertainment, adding a new area of expertise, or simply interested in how the business looks from another perspective, think about the value of doing another internship somewhere down the road. It could be the start of something big.

# Index